I CAN MAKE A DIFFERENCE

10 Ways I Can
Save the Earth

Sara Antill

PowerKiDS
press.
New York

Published in 2012 by The Rosen Publishing Group, Inc.
29 East 21st Street, New York, NY 10010

First Edition

Editor: Jennifer Way
Book Design: Ashley Drago

Photo Credits: Cover, pp. 6–7 Shutterstock.com; pp. 4–5 Tim Platt/Getty Images; pp. 8–9 Tim Pannell/Getty Images; p. 10 Jupiterimages/Pixland/Thinkstock; p. 11 Jupiterimages/Creatas/Thinkstock; p. 12 Stephen Swain Photography/Getty Images; p. 13 (top) Jonathan Wood/Getty Images; p. 13 (bottom) Roy Mehta/Getty Images; p. 14 Image Source/Getty Images; p. 15 Jeff Randall/Getty Images; p. 16 © www.iStockphoto.com/Catalin Petolea; p. 17 © www.iStockphoto.com/Grady Reese; p. 18 Jupiterimages/Brand X Pictures/Thinkstock; p. 19 Comstock Images/Comstock/Thinkstock; pp. 20–21 Jamie Grill/Getty Images; p. 22 © www.iStockphoto.com/Jani Bryson.

Library of Congress Cataloging-in-Publication Data

Antill, Sara.
  10 ways I can save the earth / by Sara Antill. — 1st ed.
      p. cm. — (I can make a difference)
  Includes index.
  ISBN 978-1-4488-6203-0 (library binding) — ISBN 978-1-4488-6365-5 (pbk.) —
  ISBN 978-1-4488-6366-2 (6-pack)
  1. Environmentalism—Juvenile literature. I. Title.
  GE195.5.A58 2012
  333.72—dc23
                                      2011029669

Manufactured in the United States of America

CPSIA Compliance Information: Batch #WW12PK: For Further Information contact Rosen Publishing, New York, New York at 1-800-237-9932

Contents

Keep the Earth Safe!

Many people on Earth live in ways that produce a lot of waste. All that waste is not good for the **environment**. Rivers, soil, and air can become **polluted**, or dirty. Pollution can make people, plants, and animals very sick. When an environment is not healthy, it may not be able to create new **resources** that we need to survive.

This book will show you 10 small steps that you can take to keep the Earth clean and safe. Saving the Earth may seem like a big job. However, if everybody makes a few small changes, it will make a big difference!

There are both big ways and small ways to use less energy. The wind turbines in the background make electricity from the wind, rather than by burning coal or oil. Riding a bike instead of in a car is another way to use less of the Earth's resources.

Each day we use many of Earth's natural resources. Some natural resources, such as energy from the Sun, will never run out. However, many of Earth's resources, such as trees, are limited. If we cut down trees faster than they can be regrown, someday we will run out of trees.

Look around the grocery store when you are shopping with your parents. Many of the goods that you see are packaged in **materials** such as cardboard or plastic. Try to choose goods that come with less packaging. By **reducing** the amount of resources you use, you will be helping the Earth.

When you are shopping, look at the different ways similar products are packaged. Try to pick products that use less packaging material.

2 Use It Again

How much do you throw away in a day? Maybe you bring your sandwich to school in a plastic bag or drink your juice or water from a **disposable** plastic bottle. When you

8

Cloth grocery bags can be cleaned and reused. This cuts down on the number of plastic grocery bags that get used and thrown away.

buy something from the store, you probably carry it home in a plastic shopping bag that gets thrown away.

One of the easiest ways to create less waste is to use things that last instead of things that are disposable. That way you can **reuse** them again and again without buying something new! Try bringing your lunch in reusable containers. With a little planning, you can bring an entire "waste-free" lunch!

9

3 Recycle

Paper   Glass   Cans   Plastic

Many of the things we buy come in containers that can be recycled. Taking the time to separate recyclables cuts down on the trash that goes to landfills.

Most of the trash that we produce goes to **landfills**. Some waste, like old food, will **decompose**, or break down in the soil, in a few days or weeks. Other waste, however, such as aluminum foil, can take hundreds of years to break down. Plastics and Styrofoam can take a million years to decompose!

Luckily, much of our waste can be **recycled** instead of thrown into a landfill. You can sort your recyclable waste into separate containers, labeled "paper" and "plastic and metal." Learn about the recycling rules in your town. When you buy things like notebook paper or pencils, look for goods made from recycled materials.

Find out which days recycling is collected in your town or city. It may ask that recycling be placed in special bins or in clear bags. It is important to know these rules before you put out your recycling!

4 Conserve Water

A dripping faucet wastes water. Make sure the faucet is turned off completely when you are done using it. If it is leaking, ask your parents to fix it.

It is easy to see how much trash we produce in a day. What about other kinds of waste, though? Sometimes people can waste resources, such as water, without even realizing it!

RIGHT: *As with a low-flow toilet, switching to a low-flow showerhead is another way to conserve water.*

BELOW: *A dual-flush toilet is a low-flow toilet that saves water by letting users flush liquid waste using less water than is used to flush solid waste.*

Only a small amount of the water on Earth is clean and safe to drink. You can **conserve**, or use less, water by taking shorter showers instead of baths. Talk to your parents about switching to a low-flow toilet in your house. These toilets use 1.6 gallons (6 l) of water with each flush. That is less than half the water that regular toilets use!

Here are an incandescent lightbulb (left) and a CFL (right).

It might be hard to imagine wasting energy since we cannot see it. However, the energy in our houses comes from Earth's resources, such as natural gas. Natural gas, oil, and coal are **nonrenewable** resources that will one day run out.

An easy way to use less energy in your house is by switching your lightbulbs to compact fluorescent lamps, or CFLs. These lightbulbs use 75 percent less energy than the **incandescent lightbulbs** that many people use. Switching will reduce the amount of electricity a house uses, which in turn reduces the amount of nonrenewable resources used to produce electricity.

CFLs use less energy and last much longer than incandescent lightbulbs. This means that one CFL can last for several years!

6 Eat Local

The oranges you see in the grocery store likely come from Florida and California. It takes a lot of gasoline to power the trucks that drive food all over the country. Gasoline is made from crude oil, which is a nonrenewable resource. By choosing to buy foods that are grown closer to your home, you will help reduce the amount of gasoline used.

Fruits and vegetables usually have a sticker or a sign to tell you where they came from. When you look for locally grown foods, you also learn what grows in your area at different times of the year.

 7 Eat More Veggies

It takes a lot of resources to raise animals for food. Many scientists think that if we did not raise so many animals to eat, we would have more resources to feed people all over the world. Eating less meat can be healthy for the environment and your body!

It can be fun to try new fruits and vegetables. You may even discover you have some new favorite foods!

8 Learn About Composting

Compost is a mix of matter such as leaves, grass clippings, and food scraps. People use compost in their gardens to help plants grow without using manmade **fertilizers**. Composting keeps food scraps and clippings out of the garbage so that they will not take up space in a landfill.

Compost makes the soil in your garden richer.

9 Plant a Tree

Trees are an important part of our environment. They take in a gas called carbon dioxide and release oxygen, which we need to survive. See if you can find a community group that plants trees. You can even use the compost from your compost pile to help the new trees grow strong!

Arbor Day is the last Friday in April. Many communities plant trees on this day.

Using less energy is a great way to help the Earth. It is also important to learn about energy that comes from renewable resources. Energy from the Sun, called solar energy, will never run out. Some people have solar panels on their roofs to collect energy from the Sun. These people can use this energy to power things in their homes.

This girl is holding a solar panel. You might study renewable energy resources in science class and present a report on them.

We can also use the power of the wind to get energy. Dams can gather energy from moving water. Write letters to the people who run your city or town asking them to look for new ways to gather energy that do not hurt the environment.

21

Many Helping Hands

There are many choices you can make that will help the environment. It can seem hard to make a big difference by yourself. Getting others involved can help you make a greater impact. Talk to your family about making your home more Earth friendly. See if your teacher will help you start a recycling program at your school.

Each city has its own recycling program. Learn about the rules in your city. Ask your school to set out recycling bins and encourage everyone to use them.

You and your friends can start a community garden and ask other people to bring you their yard waste for a community compost pile. By making better choices and helping those around you make better choices, you will be helping save our planet!

Glossary

compost (KOM-pohst) A mixture of decaying matter, such as leaves, used as a fertilizer.

conserve (kun-SERV) To keep something from being wasted or used up.

decompose (dee-kum-POHZ) To rot.

disposable (dih-SPOH-zuh-bel) Able to be thrown away.

environment (en-VY-ern-ment) All the living things and conditions of a place.

fertilizers (FUR-tuh-lyz-erz) Things put in soil to help crops grow.

incandescent lightbulbs (in-kun-DEH-sent LYT-bulbz) Objects that produce light when a piece inside the bulb is heated by an electric current.

landfills (LAND-filz) Places where waste is buried between layers of earth.

materials (muh-TEER-ee-ulz) What things are made of.

nonrenewable (non-ree-NOO-uh-bul) Not able to be replaced once used.

polluted (puh-LOOT-ed) Poisoned with harmful matter.

recycled (ree-SY-kuld) To have saved something to be used again instead of throwing it away.

reducing (rih-DOOS-ing) Bringing down in size or amount.

resources (REE-sawrs-ez) Supplies or sources of energy or useful things.

reuse (ree-YOOZ) To use something again.

Index

A
animals, 4, 17

C
compost, 18–19

E
energy, 6, 14–15,
  20–21
environment, 4, 17,
  19, 21–22

F
fertilizers, 18

G
gas, 14, 19

I
incandescent
  lightbulbs, 15

L
landfill(s), 10–11,
  18

P
plants, 4, 18
pollution, 4

R
resource(s), 4, 6–7,
  12, 14–17, 20

S
soil, 4, 10
Sun, 6, 20

T
trees, 6, 19

W
waste, 4, 9–12, 22
water, 8, 12–13, 21

Web Sites

Due to the changing nature of Internet links, PowerKids Press has developed an online list of Web sites related to the subject of this book. This site is updated regularly. Please use this link to access the list: www.powerkidslinks.com/diff/earth/